W9-AVO-578

The Praying Mantis

This book has been reviewed
for accuracy by
Walter L. Gojmerac
Professor of Entomology
University of Wisconsin—Madison.

Library of Congress Cataloging in Publication Data

Pohl, Kathleen.
  The praying mantis.

  (Nature close-ups)
  Adaptation of: Kamakiri / Jun Nanao.
  Summary: Discusses the life cycle and habitat of
the praying mantis.
   1. Praying mantis—Juvenile literature.   [1. Praying
mantis]   I. Nanao, Jun. Kamakiri.   II. Title.
III. Series.
QL508.M2P64   1986   595.7′25   86-26259

ISBN 0-8172-2715-6 (lib. bdg.)
ISBN 0-8172-2733-4 (softcover)

This edition first published in 1987 by Raintree Publishers Inc.

1 2 3 4 5 6 7 8 9 0   90 89 88 87 86

15542

The Praying Mantis

Adapted by
Kathleen Pohl

Raintree Publishers
Milwaukee

The praying mantis is sometimes called the dragon of the insect world because it is such a fierce hunter, or predator. An adult mantis will attack butterflies, bees, beetles, or other mantises, and even animals much larger than itself—frogs, lizards, and small birds.

The mantis has two forelegs covered with sharp spines. It uses them as deadly weapons. The mantis reaches out its forelegs with lightning speed to catch its victims, or prey.

When it is not hunting, the praying mantis usually keeps its forelegs folded in front of it, as if it were praying. That is why it is called the praying mantis.

There are about 1,700 kinds, or species, of mantises in the world. Most live in warm, tropical climates. Only a few species live in the United States. One native species is commonly called the Carolina mantis. The species described in this book is a Chinese mantis. Its Latin name is *Tenodera sinensis*. It is believed to have been brought to the United States on a shipment of imported goods around 1900.

▶ A praying mantis has just caught a large, brown cicada.

Sometimes a mantis hangs upside-down on a branch as it eats heavy insects.

◀ **An ootheca on a pussy willow stem.**

The ootheca of the praying mantis is about the size of a walnut. Its brown color blends with the color of the plant stem. This helps keep it hidden from enemies.

▶ **A cross-section of an ootheca.**

The praying mantis eggs are laid in rows, each egg in its own tiny room. The hardened foam protects the eggs from the winter cold.

In fall, the female praying mantis prepares to lay her eggs. She chooses a sturdy plant stem or branch on which to form an egg case, called an ootheca. She squeezes out a thick, white substance from the back part of her body, the abdomen. Then the mantis whips this toothpaste-like substance into a froth. The froth contains air bubbles that form tiny rooms around the eggs as she lays them. She may lay as many as 300 eggs.

The frothy egg case quickly hardens and turns brown. The mantis eggs remain inside the ootheca through the winter. The tough, outer shell of the egg case protects the eggs from the cold, harsh winds of winter, and from animals that search for mantis eggs to eat.

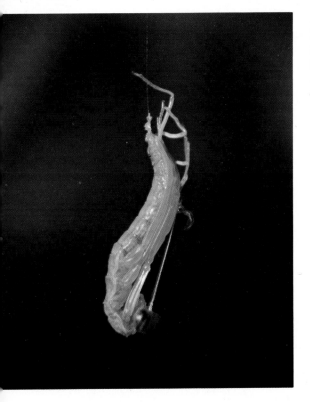

▲ A nymph covered by a film of skin.　　　▲ A nymph that has shed its membrane.

Inside the eggs, tiny mantis nymphs are developing. Those that survive the cold of winter and the watchful eye of predators emerge from, come out of, the egg case in the spring.

The ootheca begins to soften in the warm spring sunshine. Soon, hundreds of tiny, yellow mantis nymphs begin to break through the lower part of the ootheca. At first, the nymphs dangle upside-down from the ootheca, still attached to it by a slender, white thread. Each nymph is encased in a clear sac of skin, or membrane. The nymphs wriggle around inside the membranes to free themselves. They wait for their bodies to stretch and dry. Then they reach out with their long legs and begin to march along the plant stem.

◀ Hundreds of praying mantis nymphs emerging from the ootheca.

The mantis nymph is tiny at first, about the size of a mosquito. It looks very much like an adult mantis, except that it is smaller, lighter in color, and does not yet have wings.

The lives of the mantis nymphs are filled with danger. As soon as they break out of the ootheca, many nymphs are eaten by ants, birds, spiders, and other hungry predators. Many others are drowned in spring rains.

Mantis nymphs usually emerge from the egg case at night, when they are more likely to be hidden from enemies.

◄ **Newly emerged nymphs.**

These mantis nymphs are marching single file along a plant stem.

▶ **A mantis nymph caught by an ant.**

The black ant is one of the worst enemies of the mantis nymph. Ants seem to know instinctively when the nymphs will emerge from the ootheca. They are probably also attracted to the nymphs' scent.

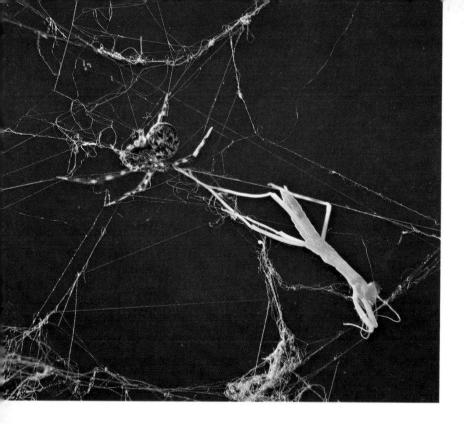

▲ A mantis nymph caught in a cobweb.

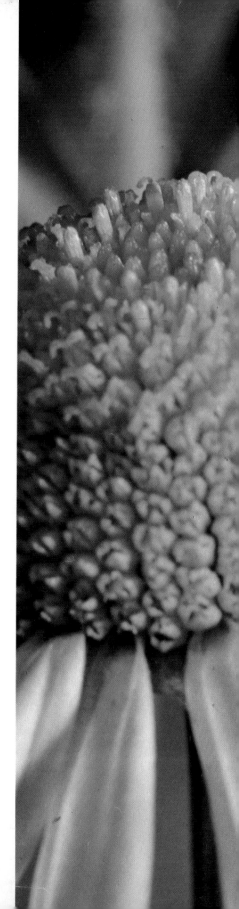

The adult mantis has few enemies because it is such a fierce hunter itself. But the tiny nymphs are preyed upon by many animals. Sometimes the nymphs play dead to discourage predators, like spiders, that generally only attack moving objects. It is one of the few ways the nymph is able to defend itself. Of all the nymphs that emerge from the ootheca, only a few will survive to become adult mantises.

▶ A nymph pretending to be dead.

▲ A mantis nymph watching a leafhopper.

Praying mantises are carnivores, which means they are meat-eaters. The nymphs hunt, or prey upon, insects smaller than themselves—leafhoppers, aphids, and very small flies. Like the adults, the mantis nymphs use their spiny forelegs to reach out with lightning speed to catch their prey. The mantis almost always bites its victim behind the head to paralyze it. Then the mantis eats its prey.

The mantis's two pairs of hind legs are very long and slender, making it easy for the insect to move through the tall grass as it stalks its prey. The legs have claws at the tips for holding onto the slippery surface of plant stems and leaves.

Mantises are usually green or brown in color. Their color helps them to blend in with their surroundings. So the mantis often hides on a plant stem or in the grass and waits for a victim to come near.

▲ A nymph that has just caught its prey.

The mantis supports its body weight on its four back legs while its front legs reach out to grasp its prey.

▶ A nymph eating its prey.

The mantis's spiny front legs are hinged. They can snap together like the blade of a jackknife to catch insects.

◀ **A mantis nymph whose body color has darkened.**

The green color of this nymph helps keep it hidden from enemies. It blends in with the green grass and the plant stems around it.

▶ **A mantis nymph molting.**

Usually the nymph molts on a quiet evening when there is little wind and it can stay hidden from enemies.

The mantis nymph eats a great deal during the summer. It grows quickly. But its hard, outer skin, called an exoskeleton, does not grow with it. So the nymph must shed its old skin, or molt, from time to time.

When it molts, the mantis hangs upside-down from a plant stem. Then its old skin splits down the back. The mantis slowly works its body out of the old, tight-fitting skin. First its head appears. Then comes the mantis's thorax, or mid-section, with the three pairs of legs. Finally, the long, segmented abdomen is pulled from the old skin.

Molting is a dangerous time for the mantis nymph. It cannot move during the process, so it is easy prey to birds and other predators.

Mantis nymphs may molt five to ten times in all, depending on the species. They grow larger with each molt. Their body color looks more and more like that of the adult mantis.

The bigger the mantis nymph becomes, the more food it needs. It begins to feed on larger insects, such as butterflies, horseflies, and beetles. By the end of the summer, the mantis may be four or five inches long. Because of its large size and its forelegs which serve as such a deadly weapon, the mantis is able to attack small birds, frogs, toads, and lizards.

▶ A mantis that has just caught a butterfly.

▼ A praying mantis watching a horsefly.

In the later molts, tiny wing pads appear on either side of the nymph's thorax. But these do not appear as actual wings until the mantis's final molt. Then the wrinkled wings are unfolded and stretched out to dry. The wings are pale at first, but they darken as they begin to dry. There are two pairs of wings. The upper pair is longer and more slender than the lower, wider wings. When this final molt is complete, the praying mantis has become a winged adult.

Because the mantis goes through definite physical changes as it develops, it is said to go through a metamorphosis. The word *metamorphosis* means "change." The praying mantis goes through three stages: egg, nymph, and adult. Scientists call this an incomplete metamorphosis because the nymph looks quite a lot like the adult insect. Some other insects, like butterflies and moths, go through four stages of development: egg, larva, pupa, and adult. In the larval stage, the insect does not look at all like the adult. Scientists call this a complete metamorphosis.

▲ **The nymph's wing pads.**

The wings of the mantis are forming inside the tiny wing pads.

▶ **A praying mantis in its final molt.**

During the final molt, the mantis's wings appear. At first, they are wrinkled and pale. Soon they are stretched out and begin to dry.

Praying mantises are not very good fliers, even though they have two pairs of wings. Usually only the males fly. They look awkward in flight, with their abdomens and long legs outstretched. Male mantises fly slowly and cover only short distances.

In the fall of the year, you may see male mantises fluttering above the tall field grass, looking for mates. Some other kinds of insects, like crickets and grasshoppers, can make sounds to attract females to them. But the male mantis cannot. His long, slender front wings and fanlike back wings carry him in the air as he searches for a female mantis in the grass below.

◄ **A praying mantis flying.**

The praying mantis looks heavy and awkward in flight.

◄ A mantis threatening an enemy.

When a mantis feels threatened, it fans out its wings so it seems larger and more frightening. This mantis's forelegs are held in the praying position.

▶ A mantis lying in wait for a black-horned katydid.

The mantis is hanging upside-down on the plant stem. The katydid is above it. Female mantises eat a lot in late summer and early fall to nourish the eggs they carry in their bodies.

The female praying mantis cannot fly because her body is so heavy with the eggs she carries in her abdomen. But she does make use of her wings to scare off enemies. When she spreads her wings to make herself look larger and fiercer, she looks like a tiny, winged dragon.

The praying mantis's head is shaped like a triangle. It is broad at the top and pointed at the chin. The mantis can turn its head in many directions. It is the only insect that can look back, as if it is looking over its shoulder. The mantis has two large compound eyes. Each one is made up of thousands of tiny lenses. They detect movement. And it has three tiny, simple eyes, called ocelli. Scientists believe they respond mostly to light. The mantis uses its two long feelers, or antennae, to detect odor and movement.

Praying mantises, like their relatives, grasshoppers and katydids, mate in the fall of the year. When a male praying mantis finds a female, he must be very careful as he comes near her. If the female spies him moving, she may attack him, even if they are members of the same species. Once the male is attacked, he cannot defend himself because the female is larger and stronger than he is. So the male cautiously approaches the female from behind.

Then the male praying mantis climbs onto the female's back and they mate. He gives her sperm, which join with her eggs, fertilizing them. From them, baby mantises will be born.

Often, the female mantis eats the male after the two have mated. He has become just another food source for her. Sometimes she may even begin to eat him during the mating process.

▶ **Two praying mantises mating.**

By late fall, the female's abdomen is swollen with eggs. The male approaches her from behind so she will not be able to attack him.

◄ A dead mantis.

The female mantis may make several oothecae and lay several batches of eggs in the fall before she dies.

► An ootheca in winter.

The ootheca looks like a bump on the plant stem. It protects the eggs from snow and cold. But sometimes, woodpeckers or squirrels tear apart oothecae to eat the mantis eggs.

After she has mated, the female mantis begins to make her ootheca and lay her eggs. Soon after this task is completed, she dies. But the eggs she has laid will stay snug and warm inside the sturdy ootheca during harsh winter storms. And in the spring, many baby mantises will be born.

There have been myths and superstitions about praying mantises for centuries. The ancient Greeks believed mantises had supernatural powers. In England, mantises are called camel crickets. According to superstition there, if a person gets lost, a praying mantis will be able to point the way. Another myth has it that mantises always face east, toward Mecca, when they are in their praying position.

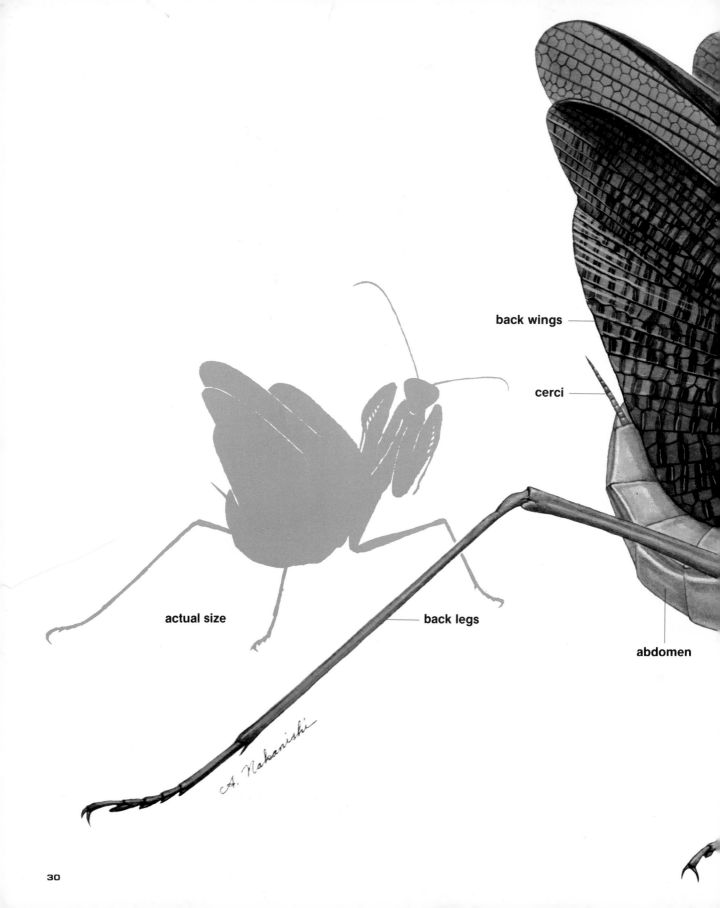

back wings

cerci

abdomen

actual size

back legs

A. Nakanishi

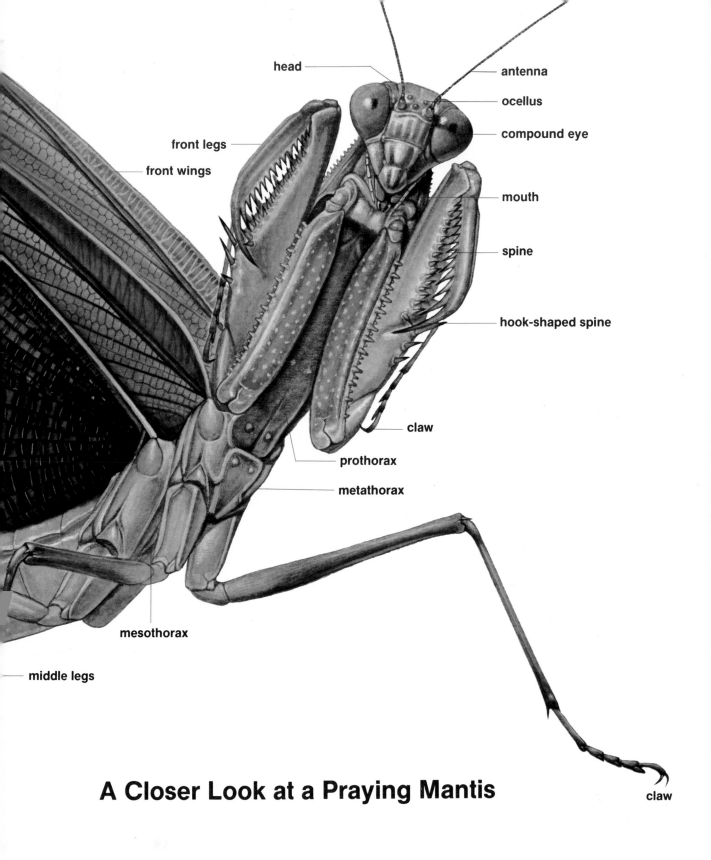

head

antenna

ocellus

compound eye

front legs

front wings

mouth

spine

hook-shaped spine

claw

prothorax

metathorax

mesothorax

middle legs

claw

A Closer Look at a Praying Mantis

GLOSSARY

antennae—the movable feelers on an insect's head that detect odor and movement. (p. 24)

carnivores—animals that eat meat. (p. 14)

compound eyes—an insect's eyes, comprised of many tiny lenses, or individual eyes. (p. 24)

exoskeleton—an insect's hard outer skin to which muscles are attached and which protects its soft, internal body parts. (p. 16)

instinct—behavior with which an animal is born, rather than behavior which is learned. (p. 11)

metamorphosis—a process of development during which physical changes take place. Complete metamorphosis involves four stages: egg, larva, pupa, and adult. Incomplete metamorphosis occurs in three stages: egg, nymph, and adult. (p. 20)

molt—to shed the outer skin. (pp. 16, 20)

ocelli—an insect's simple eyes. (p. 24)

ootheca—the hardened egg case that protects the praying mantis's eggs. (pp. 6, 9)

predators—animals that hunt and kill other animals for food. (pp. 4, 11, 12)

species—a group of animals which scientists have identified as having common traits. (p. 4)